The Solar System Glossary

 **Rotate:** to spin on its axis.

 **Satellite:** this orbits a planet. Our moon is one!

 **Saturn:** a gassy planet with an amazing ring system.

 **Solar System:** consists of a sun, planets, dwarf planets, comets, asteroids and satellites.

 **Star:** a huge ball of gas that gives out light. Our Sun is one!

 **Sun:** a burning star that gives out heat and light.

 **Tilt:** how much a line moves from the vertical.

 **Uranus:** third largest planet in our solar system. Seventh furthest from the Sun.

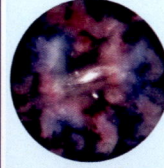 **Universe:** all of time, space and its contents.

 **Venus:** a hot planet with acidic clouds. Second closest to the Sun.

The Solar System

1   Solar System

- The word **solar** means **sun**.

- Our solar system is made up of a sun, 8 planets, a dwarf planet, comets, asteroids and satellites.

2   Where Are We?

- Our solar system is in a galaxy called **The Milky Way**.

- There are at least **two hundred billion stars** in The Milky Way.

3   The Universe

- There are approximately **one hundred billion** galaxies in the universe - that we can see so far!

The Solar System

- Read, engage and learn!
- Full colour, illustrated topic booklet.
- Glossary, Memory Map, Active Revision Game, Flashcards.
- Ideal for Common Entrance and KS3 pupils.

This Oaka™ Books Topic Booklet goes hand in hand with the Active Learning Pack on this topic. The pack also includes a Write Your Own Notes Booklet, an Active Learning Game and Question & Answer flashcards.

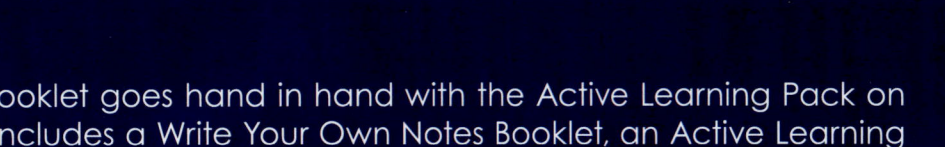

Fresh Focus on Learning

Oaka™
BOOKS

The Solar System Glossary

 **Asteroids:** small, rocky masses orbiting the Sun.

 **Axis:** the centre line around which a planet rotates.

 **Earth:** our home, the third planet from the Sun.

 **Eclipse:** when the moon casts a shadow on the Earth.

 **Eliptical (or an elipse):** oval or egg-shaped.

 **Galaxy:** a group of millions of stars.

 **Jupiter:** huge gassy planet with a giant red spot.

 **Luminous:** something that gives out light.

 **Mars:** a red planet with canyons, volcanoes and remains of polar ice caps.

 **Mercury:** the planet nearest to the Sun.

 **The Milky Way:** the galaxy that contains our solar system.

 **Neptune:** a blue planet. One of the most gassy planets in our solar system.

 **Orbit:** the path of a planet around the Sun, or a satellite around a planet.

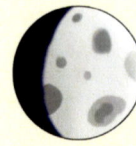 **Phase:** the part of a moon or planet that we can see at a certain time.

 **Planet:** this orbits a star and reflects the star's light.

 **Pluto:** a dwarf planet. Usually furthest from the Sun.

4 How Big?

- As telescopes get better, we can see more and more **galaxies**.

5 The Sun

- The **Sun is the largest object** in our solar system.

- All the planets in our solar system **orbit** the Sun.

I'm the biggest object in the solar system!

6 Light

- **Sun is a burning star** that emits (gives out) light.

- We can see the planets and moons in our solar system.

- This is because the light from the Sun is **reflected** off them.

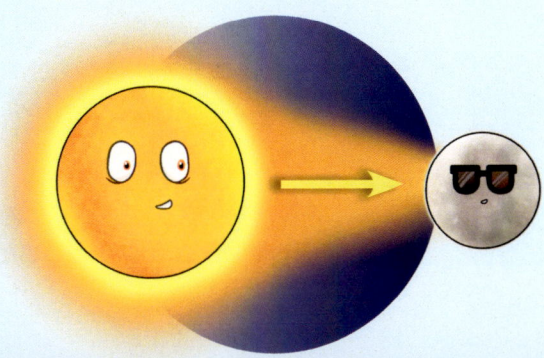

7 Heat

- The Sun is about **14 million degrees Celsius** at its center.

- It is the **source** of most life on this planet.

I'm hot stuff AND so important!

Distance in the Solar System

8 How Long Is A Year?

- **One year** is the time that it takes for a planet to complete **one orbit** around the Sun.

- The further the planet is away from the Sun, the longer the year is!

9 Order of the Planets

- There are **eight planets** that orbit our Sun.

- There used to be nine, but because **Pluto** is so small, it is now called a **dwarf planet**.

I'm now a dwarf planet!

10 Learning The Planets!

Why not make up your own rhyme?

This will help you learn the order of the planets away from the Sun!

My	Mercury
Very	Venus
Easy	Earth
Method	Mars
Just	Jupiter
Speeds	Saturn
Up	Uranus
Naming	Neptune

Days in the Solar System

11   Quicker on Mercury!

- A **year on Mercury** (the closest planet to the Sun), lasts about **88 Earth days!**

- A **year on Neptune** (the furthest planet from the Sun), lasts about **60,190 Earth days!**

I have the shortest years!

I have the longest years!

12   Axis

- Planets spin on their **axis**.

- The axis may be upright or tilted.

- The tilt on the **Earth's axis**, is **23 degrees**.

I'm wonky!

13   How Long Is A Day?

- One day is the time that it takes for a planet to complete one spin on its axis.

- The slower the planet spins, the longer the day lasts!

14   Question Time!

- A school day on Venus would last about 250 times longer than ours!

- Does this mean Venus spins faster or slower than the Earth?

- A school day on Saturn, would last about half as long as ours!

- Does Saturn spin faster or slower than the Earth?

15   Day and Night

daytime

Light rays

night time

As the Earth spins, **one side** of it **faces the Sun.**

That side is **daytime.**

The other side is in darkness.

That side is **night time!**

16   Temperature On Our Planet

It is **hottest** where the **Sun's rays** hit the Earth **vertically.**

at an angle

vertically

at an angle

Where the Sun's rays hit the Earth at an **angle**, it receives much **less** heat.

The Length of an Earth Day

The Earth takes 24 hours to spin on its axis. This is one Earth day!

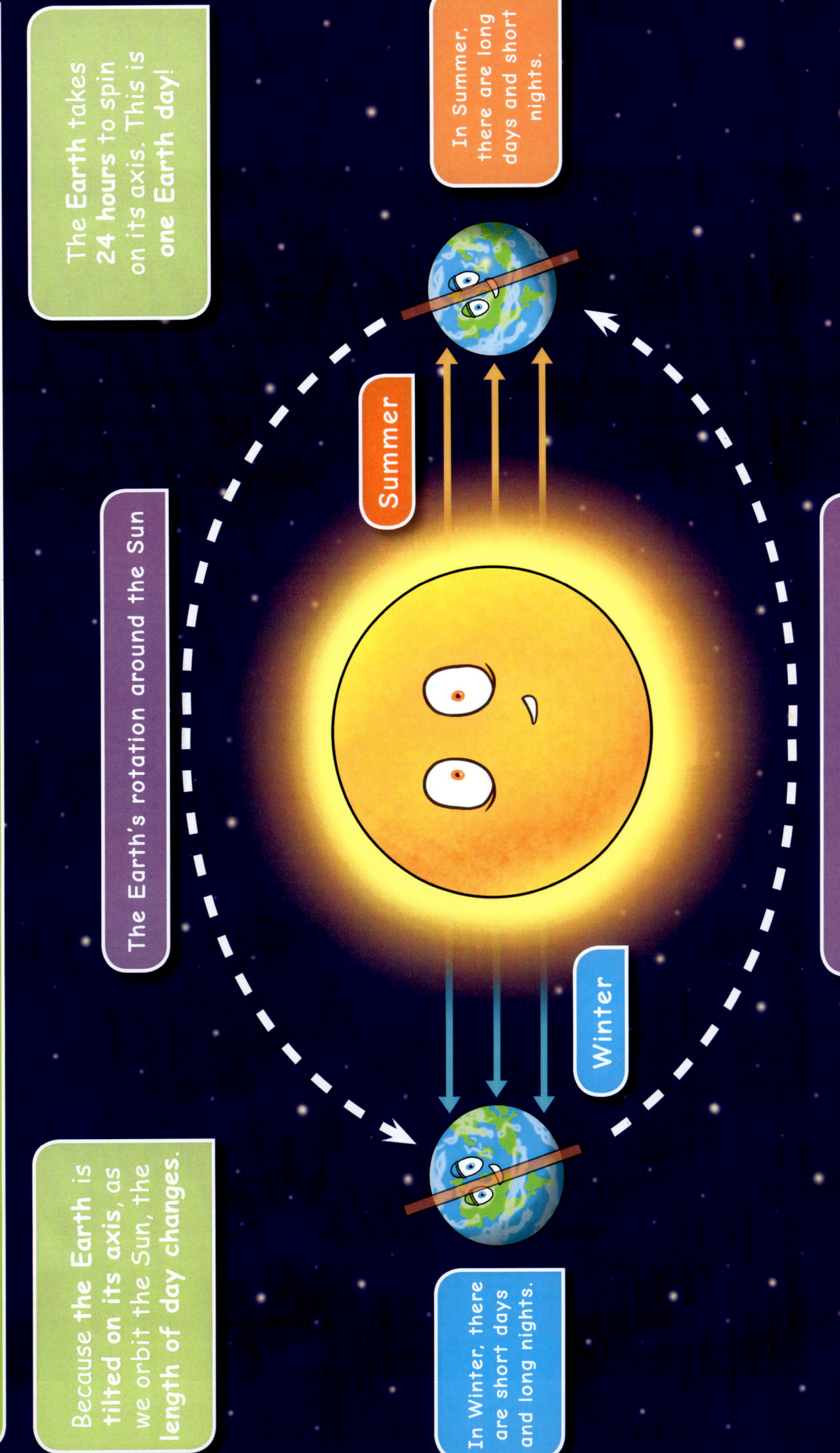

The Earth's rotation around the Sun

In Summer, there are long days and short nights.

Summer

Winter

The Earth's rotation around the Sun

Because the Earth is tilted on its axis, as we orbit the Sun, the length of day changes.

In Winter, there are short days and long nights.

17 Orbiting

- The four **closest** planets to the sun are called **terrestrial** planets.

- This means they are **like Earth**.

- These four rocky planets have nearly perfect **circular orbits**.

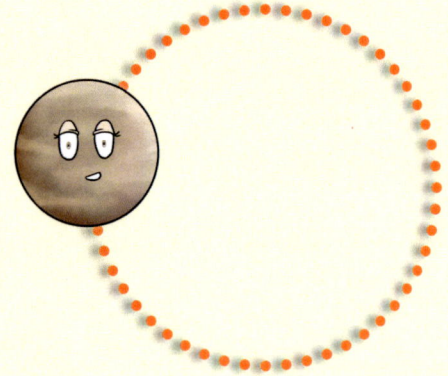

18 Orbiting

- The larger outer four planets (known as **gas giants**) have **elliptical orbits**.

- Elliptical orbits are where the planet orbits in an **oval shape**, not in a perfect circle.

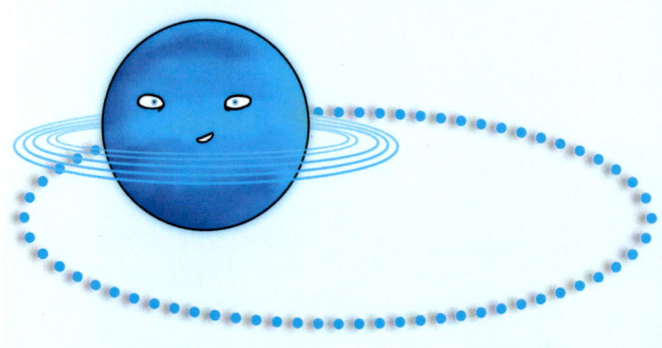

19 The Seasons

- The **seasons** we have and the **temperature** depends on where you live on this planet.

- The **North** and **South Poles never** point directly at the **Sun**. This means they will never be hot.

- The hottest countries lie near or on the **equator**, like South Africa and Australia.

- They spend much of their time pointing directly at the Sun.

Orbiting

20

The Moon Orbiting Earth

The **Moon** is a natural **satellite** that **orbits** our planet.

I'm not letting go of you!

gravity

The **gravity** from the Earth holds the Moon in its orbit.

21

The Sun's Gravity

The **gravity** from **the** Sun holds all the **planets** in their **orbits**.

Note how the orbits change shape.

22 The Tides

- **Gravity** from the **Moon** pulls on the **oceans** of our planet.

- It makes the oceans **bulge** up.

- As the Earth **spins** on its axis, the oceans are **bulged** in different areas.

- This makes the **tides rise and fall** every 12 hours.

Low Tide

High Tide

High Tide

Earth spinning

Low Tide

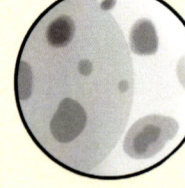

The oceans bulge out into a high tide due to the **spinning** of the Earth.

23 The Lunar Phase

- It takes the **Moon** about **28 days** to **orbit** us.

- **The Lunar Phase** is how much of the Moon can be seen from Earth.

24 The Lunar Phase

- The Lunar Phase depends on the position of the Earth, Moon and Sun.

REMEMBER!

We can only see the Moon because light from the Sun is reflected from it!

Phases of the Moon
(not tested for CE)

As the Moon orbits the Earth, we see the Moon at a **different angle**.

This makes the shape of the Moon **appear** to change.

When the Moon is on the opposite side to the Sun, the whole Moon **reflects** sunlight.

This is called a **Full Moon**.

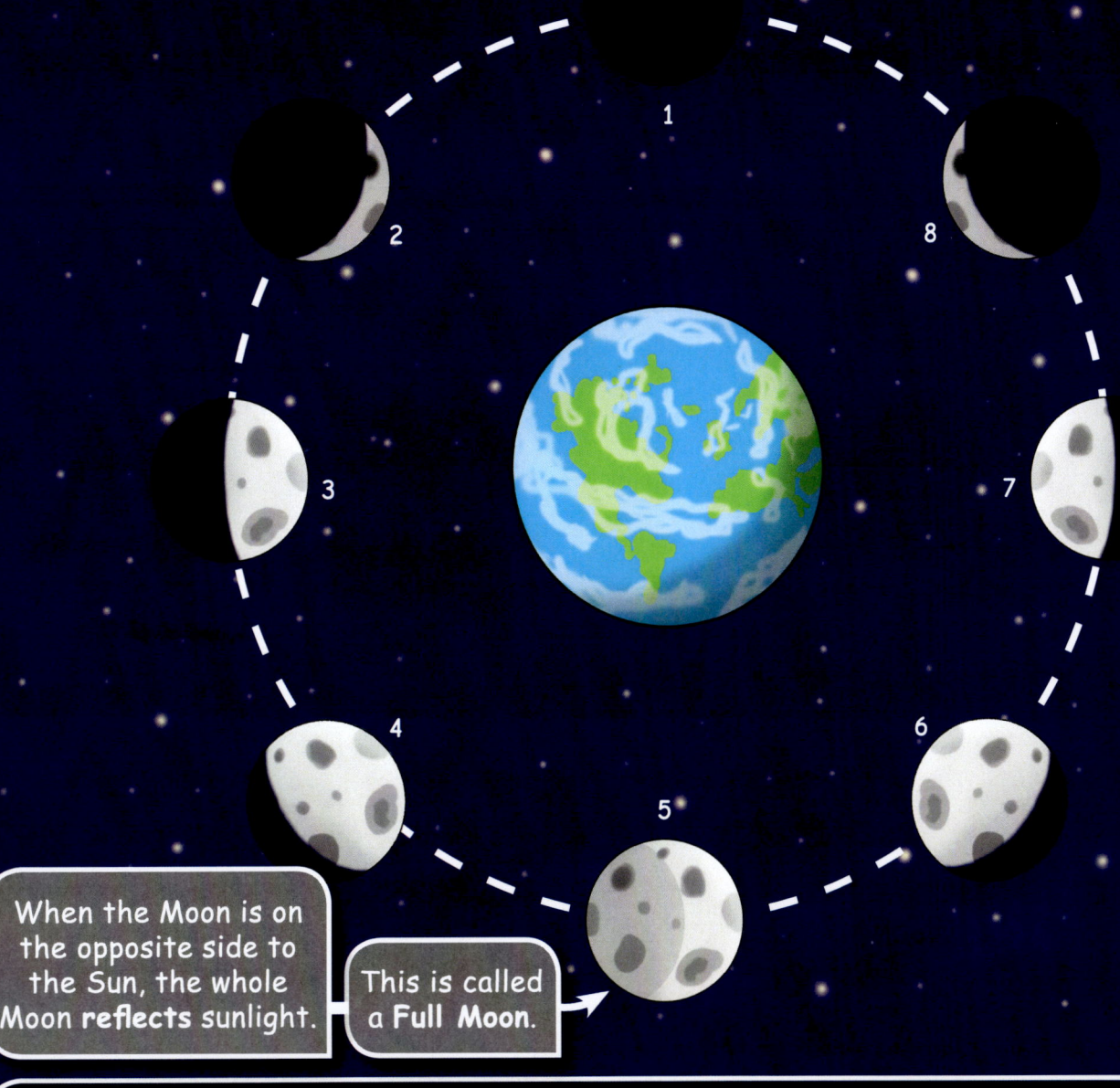

Stages of the Moon's orbit

1	2	3	4	5	6	7	8
new moon	waxing crescent	first quarter	waxing gibbous	full moon	waning gibbous	last quarter	waning crescent

Eclipses

25

A Lunar Eclipse

- A **lunar eclipse** is when the **Moon** is in the **shadow** of the **Earth**.

- It only happens during a **full Moon**, when the Sun, Earth, and Moon are **in line**.

- There can be up to **3 lunar eclipses** per year.

moon

26

A Solar Eclipse

- A **solar eclipse** happens when the Moon passes **between** the Sun and the Earth.

- The Sun is seen as a **black disc**. It glows around the edges.

- It only happens during a full Moon when the Earth, Moon and Sun are **exactly in line**.

- A total solar eclipse happens somewhere on this planet, twice every three years!

partial eclipse

total eclipse

This booklet is not to be photocopied. Thank you.

Planets in Our Solar System

(Sections 27 - 46 are not tested for CE but we think are interesting background information on this topic)

27 The Sun

- The Sun is **109 times bigger** than the Earth.

- It has an average surface **temperature** of **6,000°C**.

28 Mercury

- Mercury is less than half the size of the Earth.

- It is the closest planet to the Sun.

- It takes just **88 days** to **orbit** the **Sun**.

29 Venus

- Venus is about the **same size** as Earth.

- But it has a surface temperature of **460°C**!

30 Earth

- Earth is **70% water**, with an atmosphere that contains **oxygen**.

- It has an average surface temperature of **24°C**.

- It is the only **known planet** in our solar system that can support **life**.

Planets in Our Solar System

31   Mars

- Mars is about **half** the size of Earth.

- It has **two Moons** (also known as satellites).

- It would take astronauts **nine months** to reach Mars!

32   Jupiter

- Jupiter is about **11 times bigger** than Earth, and it has **28 Moons**!

- It is the first of the **Gas Giants**.

- A day on Jupiter is just 10 hours long but its year is nearly 12 Earth years long!

33   Saturn

- Saturn is **10 times bigger** than Earth and it has **62 Moons** and **30 rings**!

- The surface of Saturn is **liquid hydrogen**.

34   Uranus

- Uranus is titled **98°** on its axis, more than any other main planet.

- It has a surface temperature of **-200°C**.

Planets in Our Solar System

35 Neptune

- Gravity on Neptune is nearly the **same** as on Earth.

- Neptune has 8 Moons and 5 rings.

36 Pluto

- Pluto is a **dwarf planet** about 1/5 the size of Earth.

- It is **5,914 million kilometres away** from the Sun.

37 Dwarf Planets

- **Dwarf** planets are planets **smaller** than Mercury.

- The first five recognised dwarf planets are **Ceres, Pluto, Eris, Makemake and Haumea.**

38 Comets

- Most comets are just a few kilometres in diameter.

- **Comets** are made of **ice**, **dust**, and small pieces of **rock**.

Comets, Satellites and Asteroids!

39 Halley's Comets

- When comets pass close to the Sun, the heat **vapourises** the ice.

- This creates a **trail of dust particles**.

- Halley's Comet can be seen from Earth every 75 to 76 years!

40 Satellites

- **Satellites** are moons, planets, or machines that **orbit a planet or star**.

- Earth is one of the Sun's satellites.

- The Moon is the Earth's satellite.

41 Asteroids

- Asteroids are **small, rocky masses** that orbit the Sun.

- If all the asteroids were joined together, they would still not be as big as our Moon.

42 Asteroid Belt

- The **asteroid belt** is a doughnut-shaped ring between the orbits of **Mars** and **Jupiter**.

Recent News!

 43 Pluto Photographs

- In **July 2015**, NASA announced new photos of Pluto.

- The photos were sent from the spacecraft, New Horizons.

- The recent photo shows that there are mountains rising as high as 11,000 feet!

 44 Pluto Photographs

- The photos showed two moons (out of the **five moons** that **orbit Pluto**).

- The two moons are called **Nix** and **Hydra**.

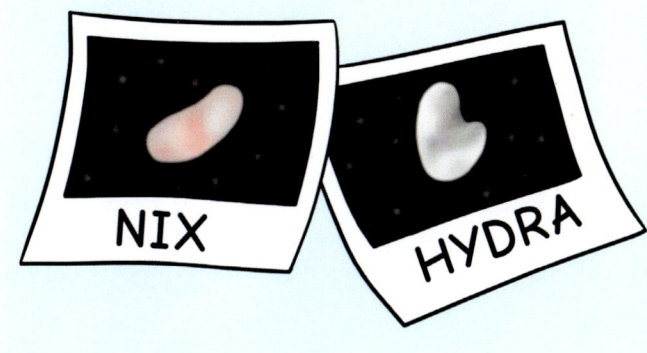

NIX   HYDRA

 45 Living On Mars

- There is a mission for humans to live on Mars. This is called **Mars One**.

- In 2013, people from all over the world applied to be a part of this mission.

People are going to live on me?!

46 Living On Mars

- It is still in the early stages of planning, but the aim is to have **humans living on Mars**.

- Their homes will be **unit pods**!

About Oaka Books

Children learn best when they are engaged...

Our aim is to help children enjoy learning by making it fun! That way they will succeed.

Following Common Entrance and National Curriculum guidelines for KS3.

Design and layout of our books follow guidelines from the British Dyslexia Association

Three Easy Steps

Read: the easy to follow bullet point Topic Booklet.

Engage: Play the Active Learning Game.

Learn: When you understand the topic, test yourself using the Write Your Own Notes Book. You can use the Topic Booklet to help if you get stuck.

One (short) Topic at a time:

For some students, a big book is a big turn off. That's why we focus on one topic at a time. Short and to the point.

Reading Age

This booklet is suitable for children with a reading age of 10 ½ years.

Topic Packs for KS1, KS2 & KS3 Include:

History
Geography
Chemistry
Biology
Physics

First paperback edition printed 2015 in the United Kingdom.
A catalogue record for this book is available from the British Library.

ISBN 978-1-909892-85-9

Designed, set and published by Oaka™ Books.

To order other titles from Oaka™ Books, please email info@oakabooks.co.uk or visit www.oakabooks.co.uk, or phone: +44 (0) 2392 388 519.

Acknowledgements
Our huge thanks go to the many teachers who have been involved in the development of this series of learning guides. Special thanks to Joy Gardiner, for producing hundreds of illustrations, to Kate Doehren, for her enthusiasm and invaluable assistance to my wonderful daughter Sophie, for being the inspiration for the books and, of course, to Charlie, for believing in them.

ISBN 978-1-909892-85-9
9 781909 892859

CE/KS3
The Solar System

Topic Booklet

ISBN 978-1-909892-85-9   Produced in association with Kate Doehren, MA Ed, B.Ed Hons, RSA Dip, Sp LD/Dyslexia
Director of Learning Support, Hurstpierpoint College
© Copyright Oaka™ Books 2018